KETO DIET FOR B

*An ultimate keto diet guide with basic
ingredients and easy recipes for weight loss*

By

Rositsa Katsarova

TABLE OF CONTENTS

Introduction 5

Chapter 1: The Ketogenic Diet 7

Chapter 2: Benefits of The Ketogenic Diet.................. 11

Chapter 3: Foods to Eat and Avoid 14

Chapter 4: Tips and Guidelines 21

Chapter 5: Breakfast Recipes 32

Chapter 6: Lunch Recipes 50

Chapter 7: Dinner Recipes 68

Chapter 8: Snack Recipes 89

Chapter 9: Side Dishes... 106

Chapter 10: Desserts 126

Conclusion.. 142

Introduction

Are you struggling to lose weight? Do you want to lose body fat without extra effort and difficulty? Then this Ketogenic diet cookbook is for you. This guide takes an easy-to-understand approach and provides everything you need to live a happier and healthier life. The Ketogenic diet is a powerful weight-loss tool that has been proven to help people lose weight quickly and easily.

In addition, the diet can fight off disease, boost your energy levels, and make you feel healthier. The Ketogenic diet is a scientifically proven low carb, moderate protein, and high-fat diet that guarantees that you will lose weight. If you want to lose weight without a high-cost plan, then the Ketogenic diet is for you. Whether you are just starting your weight loss journey or have experience with low-carb recipes before, this Ketogenic diet cookbook will put you on the path to optimal health and wellness. You are living a busy life, and sticking to your diet can be hard.

However, this Ketogenic cookbook helps you stay on track with recipes that need ingredients that are commonly available in your local grocery store. This keto book is the ultimate guide to learning everything about the Ketogenic diet to get started, achieve your weight loss results, and feel better from the inside out. Keto is now easier, simpler, and yummier than ever with this Ketogenic diet cookbook. This complete Keto diet book takes a holistic approach. With the help of this book, you can build good habits, achieve lasting weight loss results, and live a healthier, happier life.

Chapter 1

The Ketogenic Diet

Calorie Distribution on a Ketogenic Diet

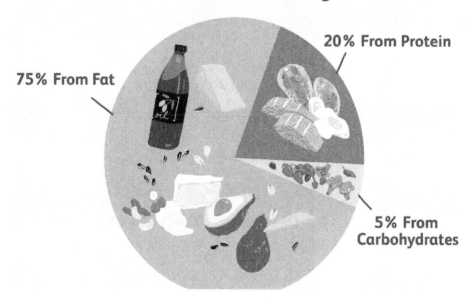

20% From Protein

75% From Fat

5% From Carbohydrates

The Ketogenic diet is a very low-carb, high fat, and moderate protein diet. This diet was discovered in the 1920s by scientists working for Johns Hopkins Medical Center. Originally, the diet was discovered to combat epilepsy in children. The keto diet works by eliminating glucose that is found in carbohydrate foods.

Sugar burner vs. fat burner

The main goal of the keto diet is to strictly limit the intake of all foods with sugar and starch (carbohydrates). Once we eat them, these foods are converted into sugar in our blood. If the sugar levels become too high, additional calories are deposited as body fat and result in undesirable weight gain. However, when glucose or sugar levels are severely restricted because of low-carb intake, the body begins to burn fat for energy and generates ketones.

Keto diets work through the removal of glucose. Because most of us eat a high-carb diet, our bodies generally depend on glucose/ sugar for energy. The human body cannot make glucose. It only has about 24 hours' worth of stored glucose in its liver and muscle tissue. Once glucose is used up, and we restrict eating carb-rich foods, the human body starts to burn body fat or fat from our food.

So when you start a Ketogenic diet plan, your body starts to burn body fat for energy instead of carbohydrates. This process helps people to lose body fat quickly, even when they are eating a lot of fat.

What is Ketosis?

Your body reaches nutritional Ketosis when you severely limit carb consumption. As a result, your body is deprived of glucose. This forces your body to burn body fat and reach Ketosis. Your body reaches Ketosis when you start to take fat as the main source of energy instead of carbohydrates.

HOW DOES KETOSIS WORK?

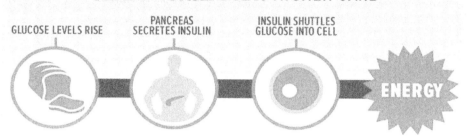

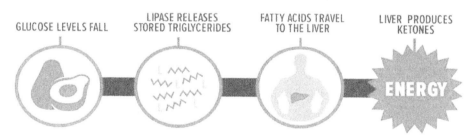

This process of using fat as fuel generates ketone bodies in your body. Once your body reaches nutritional Ketosis, your blood triglycerides levels go down. Your blood sugar and insulin levels also go down. Good cholesterol levels increase, and fat around your major organs diminishes.

Following a Ketogenic diet shifts your body into a permeant state of Ketosis. Following a Ketogenic eating style puts you into a state of Ketosis. This means that your body is converting enough fat for energy so that there are ketones present in your bloodstream.

This happens when you follow a low-carb, high-fat, moderate-protein eating plan. Being in Ketosis is a normal metabolic stage. Becoming keto-adapted is one of the goals of the Ketogenic diet. Keto adapted means your body is functioning with very little glucose.

Chapter 2

Benefits of The Ketogenic Diet

The Ketogenic diet offers various health benefits, including:

1. Lower your food and sugar cravings: This is one of the initial and the best benefit of the diet. The existence of ketone in your body will naturally lower your appetite, and fat has a very satisfying and filling presence. The ketogenic diet will be very useful in preventing your food or sugar addiction. This study shows that the diet leads to an automatic reduction in appetite.

   • https://pubmed.ncbi.nlm.nih.gov/17228046/

2. Lower blood pressure: A low-carb diet is very effective against blood pressure. Within a few weeks, you will stabilize your blood pressure and lower medication dosages. These two studies reveal that the diet leads to a reduced risk of high blood pressure.

   • https://pubmed.ncbi.nlm.nih.gov/17228046/

   • https://pubmed.ncbi.nlm.nih.gov/17341711/

3. Lower your risk of heart disease: Triglycerides are fat molecules, and excess presence of triglycerides in your blood, especially in the morning, accelerates your risk of developing heart disease. These studies prove that the diet dramatically lowers blood triglycerides.

- https://jamanetwork.com/journals/jamainternalmedicine/fullarticle/217514

- https://academic.oup.com/jn/article/136/2/384/4664306?login=true

4. Lower cholesterol: Excess glucose through diet causes your bad cholesterol levels to rise. With the Keto diet, you will consume less glucose-producing food, so your bad cholesterol levels will go down, and good cholesterol levels will go up. These three studies prove it:

- https://academic.oup.com/ajcn/article/70/6/992/4729106

- https://pubmed.ncbi.nlm.nih.gov/1386252/

- https://academic.oup.com/ajcn/article/77/5/1146/4689813?login=true

5. More energy: Following the keto diet helps to increase your energy levels. If you suffer from chronic fatigue symptoms, the diet will lower your symptoms.

6. Prevent tooth decay and gum disease: Consuming sugar-rich foods increase pH levels in your mouth and cause tooth decay

and gum disease. With this diet, you will prevent any tooth or gum-related problems.

7. Lift your mood: Various studies reveal that the existence of ketone in your body is beneficial in stabilizing the neurotransmitters such as serotonin and dopamine.

8. Help reverse type 2 diabetes: The Keto diet effectively lowers blood sugar and insulin levels and treat and help reverse type 2 diabetes. These two studies discuss more:

    - https://nutritionandmetabolism.biomedcentral.com/articles/10.1186/1743-7075-2-34
    - https://pubmed.ncbi.nlm.nih.gov/16403234/

9. Weight loss: Importantly, following the Keto diet help you to lower weight. Along with weight control, the diet will help you to reverse insulin resistance. These studies show that the diet causes rapid weight loss within the first two weeks.

    - https://pubmed.ncbi.nlm.nih.gov/12430970/
    - https://journals.physiology.org/doi/full/10.1152/ajprenal.00149.2007

10. This study is revealing that the diet is very effective in reducing harmful belly fat. It is the extra belly fat that leads to heart disease and type 2 diabetes.

    - https://nutritionandmetabolism.biomedcentral.com/articles/10.1186/1743-7075-1-13

Chapter 3

Foods to Eat and Avoid

Now we are going to discuss what you can eat and have to avoid on a Ketogenic diet. You can eat from the following food groups:

- Fats and Oils: Get your fats from meat and nuts. Supplement with monounsaturated and saturated fats like olive oil, butter, and coconut oil.

- Protein: Whenever possible, eat grass-fed, pasture-raised, organic meat. Eat meat in moderation.

- Vegetables: Focus on eating vegetables that grow above the ground, mainly leafy green vegetables.

- Dairy: Focus on buying full-fat dairy products.

- Nuts and seeds: Eat fat-rich nuts such as almonds and macadamia.

- Beverages: Stick to drinking mostly water. You can flavor it with lemon/ lime juice and stevia-based flavorings.

Let's discuss this in detail

Fats and Oils

- Saturated fats: Consume lard, coconut oil, ghee, and butter.

- Monounsaturated fats: avocado, olive, and macadamia nut oils.

- Polyunsaturated fats: Eat naturally producing polyunsaturated fats such as fatty fish and fat from animal protein. Avoid processed polyunsaturated fat such as margarine spreads.

- Trans fats: Completely avoid.

Protein

Here are the best proteins for you

- Fish: Eat Wild-caught fish like trout, snapper, salmon, mackerel, halibut, cod, tuna, and catfish. Fattier fish is better.

- Shellfish: Mussels, squid, scallops, crab, lobster, oysters, clams.

- Whole eggs: Free-range from the local market.

- Beef: Fatty cuts of steak, stew meat, roasts, ground beef

- Pork: Ham, tenderloin, pork chops, pork loin, ground beef

- Poultry: Wild game, chicken, quail, pheasant, duck

- Offal/Organ: Tongue, kidney, liver, heart

- Other meat: Wild game, turkey, veal, lamb, goat

- Bacon and Sausage: Avoid sugar or extra filler added items.

- Nut Butter: Buy natural, unsweetened nuts and choose fatter versions like macadamia or almond nut butter.

Vegetables and Fruit

Mostly eat vegetables that are low in carbs and high in nutrients. Focus on cruciferous vegetables that are leafy, green, and grown above ground.

Limit the listed vegetables and fruits

- Nightshades: peppers, eggplant, and tomato

- Root vegetables: Squash, mushrooms, garlic, parsnip, and onion

- Berries: Blueberries, blackberries, and raspberries

- Citrus: Orange, lemon, and lime

- Try to avoid starchy vegetables, bananas, and potatoes

Dairy Products

Here are some examples of dairy you can eat on the Keto

- Hard Cheese, including Swiss, Parmesan, feta, aged cheddar, etc.

- Soft Cheese, including Monterey Jack, Colby, blue, brie, mozzarella, etc.

- Spreadable, including cream Fraiche, mascarpone, sour cream, cream cheese, cottage cheese, etc.

- Homemade mayonnaise

- Heavy whipping cream

- Greek yogurt

Nuts and Seeds

- Low carb, fat-rich nuts: Pecans, Brazil nuts, macadamia nuts

- A moderate carb, fat-rich nuts: Peanuts, hazelnuts, almonds, walnuts, pine nuts

- High carb nuts: Avoid cashews and pistachios because they are high in carbs.

Water and Beverages

Here is a list of beverages that Keto allows

- Water: Drink more than 8 glasses of water daily

- Broth: Broth is important for Keto dieters. They are loaded with vitamins; nutrition and help replace electrolytes.

- You can drink tea and coffee.

- Choose unsweetened variations of almond and coconut milk.

- Avoid or severely reduce diet soda.

- Flavoring such as stevia and sucralose is fine.

- Choose hard liquor and avoid beer and wine because of high carb content.

Spices

Cayenne Pepper	Chili Powder
Cinnamon	Cumin
Oregano	Basil
Cilantro	Parsley
Rosemary	Thyme

Condiments and Sauces

Keto-friendly condiments include

- Syrups flavored with acceptable sweeteners

- Unsweetened, fatty salad dressing

- Worcestershire sauce

- Horseradish

- Low or no sugar added relish

- Low or no sugar added sauerkraut

- Cage-free mayonnaise

- Hot sauce

- Mustard

- Low or no sugar added ketchup

Try to avoid pre-made condiments

Sweeteners

Keto recommended sweeteners

- Stevia.

- Sucralose.

- Erythritol.

- Monk fruit

- Xylitol in moderation

Foods to avoid

- Sugar: Typically found in ice cream, chocolate, candy, sports drinks, juice, and soda. Avoid sugar completely.

- Grains: Avoid bread, buns, rice, corn, pastries, cakes, cereal, pasta, and beer. Avoid whole grains, including quinoa, buckwheat, barley, rye, and wheat.

- Starch: Avoid vegetables like yams and potatoes and other things like muesli and oats.

- Trans Fats: Avoid them completely.

- Fruit: Avoid large fruits that are high in sugar (bananas, oranges, apples)

- Low-fat foods: Low-fat foods are high in carbs and sugar. Avoid them.

Chapter 4

Tips and Guidelines

Tips for the beginners who want to follow to keto diet plan:

- Before starting the keto diet, take some photos of yourself from all angles, and compare them in one month. The difference in body fat will encourage you to stay with the keto diet.

- One of the goals of the keto diet is to limit carbohydrate-rich foods. Ideally, your aim should be to eat less than 20g per day. Measuring your carb intake is easy, so do not worry about consuming too much carb.

- With Keto, you are consuming less carb, but be careful about eating too much protein. Consuming excess protein will cause higher levels of glucose.

- As a beginner, you should drink a cup of broth daily for the first couple of weeks. The broth will help to maintain the electrolyte balance in your body, and you will avoid the keto flu.

- Read articles, columns, and blogs about the Keto in the newspaper and on the internet. Also, read eBooks and watch videos to know as much as possible about the diet.

- The keto diet consists of 60 to 75% fat, 15 to 30% protein, and 5 to 10% Carb. The internet is a great help to you.

- You have to strictly follow the keto diet and do not break the diet plan for a day. Even if you have broken the diet plan for 1 day, you have to start from the beginning.

- Avoid root vegetables because they are loaded with the carb.

- If you are not sure about any food or food item, then check and check again before consuming it.

Tips for following the keto diet for life

Usually, following a diet plan requires dieters to avoid foods they enjoy eating. This is one of the main reasons why diet plans fail. However, if you follow the keto diet, you only have to avoid carb-rich foods. This makes it easy for you to continue with the keto diet. Here are some useful tips for you to stick to the keto diet for life:

- Develop a sleep schedule and ensure you are getting enough sleep every night. Studies have shown that people tend to eat more when they are tired or sleep-deprived. When you are sleep deprived, your body produces a hormone that forces you to eat more.

- Find a support person who can give you mental support. The person might be your friend or a family member. Having someone supportive of your cause will help you to stay focused on a diet.

- Experiment with the ingredients, and create your keto recipes, include food items you enjoy eating. Experimenting and playing around with recipes will keep you interested in the keto diet.

- Eat 5 to 6 times daily and ensure you are not too hungry any time of the day because if you are starving, you will immediately go for carb-rich foods.

- Try a variety of keto recipes every week. This will allow you to taste different foods, and you will find it easier to maintain the diet because it will be unpredictable and exciting.

- Eat fruits and vegetables as snacks instead of cookies and cupcakes. If you feel you are hungry between meals, eat some fruits, seeds, and nuts. They are nutritious and help maintain the diet.

- If you feel the need for supplements and vitamins, consult with your doctor and decide according to his/her suggestions.

- Drink lots of water. Water will help you to control cravings for foods that are not included in the keto diet. Water will also help remove toxins from your body.

Now, we are going to discuss frequently asked questions.

How long it takes to get into Ketosis?

It can take anywhere from 2 to 7 days to enter your body into Ketosis. The time depends on what you are eating, your activity levels, and your body type. The easiest way to get into Ketosis is to limit your carb intake to 20g daily, exercise on an empty stomach, and drinking plenty of water.

How to track my carb intake?

Search the internet, and you will find plenty of good sites to track your carb intake. Here is one (https://keto-calculator.ankerl.com/)

Do I need to count calories?

You don't have to worry about calories because fats and proteins will keep you full for a long period.

What about eating too much fat?

Yes, you can eat too much fat. Search online, and you will find plenty of Keto calculators that will help you calculate your macros and how much carb, proteins and fats you should consume in a day. This is a good site (https://www.ruled.me/keto-calculator/)

How much weight will I lose?

It depends on you. Your carb consumption and your activity/exercise level determine how much weight you will lose.

What are Macros, and should I count them?

Macros are short for the world macronutrients. The main three macronutrients are carb, proteins, and fats. The best way to track your macros is thinking regarding grams.

- Fats are 10% anti-Ketogenic and 90% Ketogenic.

- Proteins are 55% anti-Ketogenic and 45% Ketogenic.

- Carbs are 100% anti-Ketogenic.

Keto Calculators will help you count your actual macros. This is a good site:

(https://www.perfectketo.com/keto-macro-calculator/).

I just started the diet and felt like not worth it

The initial symptoms of the Keto diet can make things a bit difficult for a beginner like you. So drink plenty of water and broth. Eat salted nuts, deli meat, and bacon. These foods and drinks will keep you well balanced and functional.

The ultimate goal of a Ketogenic diet is to get the body into a certain metabolic state known as Ketosis. However, many people who begin the Ketogenic diet have difficulty reaching the ketosis state or remaining in the ketosis state after they get in. Common mistakes to avoid:

1. Do not be scared of fat: You want to eat more fat to lose body fat. With Keto, you take more dietary fat and fewer dietary

carbohydrates. When you eat fewer carbs and more fat, your body uses fat as energy for the body, and you lose body weight. So do not be scared of body fat.

2. Water is important: To keep your body hydrated, you need to regularly drink enough water throughout the day. Health experts recommend that you drink at least one gallon of water every day.

3. Get salty: As a first-time keto dieter, you will feel the effects of keto flu. The symptoms include fatigue, headaches, feeling feverish, etc. Do not worry; it is nothing serious. Eating more water and salt will fix the problem.

4. Too much protein isn't good: This is another reason the body goes out of the state of Ketosis. Since meat can be included in your diet, there are times when you tend to over-eat the meat dishes. Through the gluconeogenesis process, too much protein may produce glucose.

5. Sleep is essential: If you do not give the much-needed rest to your mind and body, your system will face difficulty doing things that it is supposed to do. Good quality sleep is important for controlling your stress, giving the rest of your organs, and making you feel energetic the next day.

6. Stress management: The stress hormone cortisol can increase your blood sugar levels, which hinders your weight loss plan. Practice meditation to manage your stress.

7. Do not eat the same meal every time: Do not eat the same meal every time and make your diet boring. There are so many keto-friendly recipes out there, and you just have to choose the ones that are best for you.

8. No cheat days: Remember, with Keto, there are no cheat days. This is a strict dietary regimen, and you have to stick to its guidelines if you want to maintain your weight loss goal.

Key Pillars

1. Water: water has no calories, fat, and it is nature's appetite suppressant, and it helps the body to metabolize fat, thereby helping you lose weight.

2. Fiber: Eating more fiber offers you a lot of benefits, including normalizing bowel movements, lowers blood cholesterol levels, helps control blood sugar levels, promotes healthier gut bacteria, and reduces the risk of certain cancers.

3. Sleep: The importance of sleep cannot be overstated. Among its numerous benefits include appetite regulation, reducing your calorie intake, increasing metabolism, preventing insulin resistance, and providing energy for physical activity.

4. Positive mindset: A positive mindset can help you maintain your keto diet and realize your health and fitness goals.

5. Physical activity: The health benefits of regular exercise and physical activity are hard to ignore. Exercise helps you control weight, improve your mood, and boost your energy levels.

Keto Problems and Solutions

The diet can cause a few side effects, including

- Induction Flu: Confusion, brain fog, irritability, lethargy, nausea. These symptoms are common during the first week of the diet.

The cure: salt and water. You can cure all these symptoms by getting enough water and salt into your system. Drinking broth daily is a better option.

- Leg Cramps: Leg cramps can become painful.

The cure: Get enough salt and drink plenty of fluids. Supplementing with magnesium is also a good idea. Take 3 slow-release magnesium tablets daily for the first 3 weeks.

- Constipation: Constipation is another side effect of the diet.

The cure: The cure is getting enough salt and water. Include more fiber in your diet. Milk of Magnesia can help you prevent constipation. You will find the product on Amazon.

- Bad Breath: Bad breath is another unpleasant problem.

The cure:

- Eat a bit more carb

- Get enough salt and drink enough fluid

- Maintain a good oral hygiene

- Heart palpitations

The cure: Drinking enough water and getting enough fluid is the easiest solution.

If losing weight is still difficult for you

- Do not eat excessive amounts of protein. Too much protein converts into glycogen and prevents your body from going into Ketosis.

- Do not take artificial sweeteners. Cough syrup, chewing gums, mints contain sugar and artificial sugars.

- Avoid carb-rich snacks because carb cheating is another reason for you to gain weight.

- You may be eating too many carb-rich foods. Check and lower your carb intake and include coconut oil in your diet.

- You might be eating too much fat. The diet is fat-based, but you cannot eat an unlimited amount of fat.

- Stress can cause weight gain. When you are stressed, your body generates the hormone cortisol, which makes losing weight difficult. Manage stress.

- Hormone leptin can prevent weight gain. Leptin signals your brain when to stop eating. As you lose body fat, your brain gets fewer signals from leptin. Eat fat and protein-rich foods to minimize the effect of leptin.

Tips especially for women

Women need to approach the keto diet a bit differently:

- Meats take more time to digest. So when you are having your period, eat more vegetables, broth, and sugar-free Jell-O.

- Take omega-3. Take omega-3 fats from fatty fish such as sardines, salmon, organic beef, flaxseeds, and leafy green.

- Eat yogurt because it contains "Lactobacillus acidophilus," which is important for intimate health.

- Drink Vega (whole food shake, without artificial sugar, no soy or gluten) with almond milk to help balance your hormones.

- Exercise your breast because weight loss can make your breast saggy.

- Keep your pH in check. Drink lemon water daily.

- During your periods, eat low-carb chocolates to subdue your sweet cravings.

- Take cranberry supplements.

Chapter 5

Breakfast Recipes

Breakfast Frittata

| Prep time: 10 minutes | Cook time: 30 minutes | Servings: 8 |

Ingredients

- Eggs – 5, beaten
- Egg whites – ½ cup
- Whole ricotta cheese – ½ cup
- Sea salt – ½ tsp.
- Ground mustard spice – ¼ tsp.
- Black pepper– ¼ tsp.
- Fresh spinach – ½ cup, chopped
- Bacon – 5 slices, cooked and crumbled
- Tomato – 6 slices from a medium size
- Grated cheese – ½ cup

Method

1. Preheat the oven to 400F/200C. Grease a 9-inch pie dish.
2. In a large mixing bowl, combine black pepper, ground mustard, sea salt, ricotta, egg whites, and beaten eggs. Whisk and beat all ingredients together.
3. Add crumbled bacon, spinach to the egg mixture and stir in. Pour the egg mixture into the prepared pie dish. Add the tomato slices on top.
4. Bake until the center is done and no longer liquid, about 30 minutes.

5. Remove from oven and sprinkle with cheese.
6. Cool and serve.

Nutritional Facts Per Serving

- Calories 116
- Fat 9 g
- Carb 1 g
- Protein 8 g

Keto Omelet

| Prep time: 10 minutes | Cook time: 20 minutes | Servings: 2 |

For the roasted tomatoes

- Grape tomatoes – 1 cup, halved
- Olive oil – 1 tsp.
- Kosher salt – 1 pinch
- Black pepper to taste
- Fresh thyme or oregano

For the omelet

- Eggs – 3 large
- Salt – 1/8 tsp.

- Black pepper to taste
- Baby spinach – 1 cup, sliced
- Feta cheese – 1 ounce, crumbled

Method

1. Preheat the oven to 400F/200C.
2. Place the tomatoes on a baking sheet and season with salt, pepper, and drizzle with oil and fresh herbs.
3. Roast for about 12 to 15 minutes.
4. In the meantime, in a bowl, beat the eggs with salt, pepper, and a little water.
5. Heat a skillet over medium-low heat.
6. Spray with oil and add ½ eggs.
7. Cook for 2 to 3 minutes, or until set.
8. Place on a plate and repeat with the remaining eggs.
9. To serve: place the eggs on 2 plates, top with feta, tomatoes, spinach, salt, and pepper.

Nutritional Facts Per Serving

- Calories 183
- Fat 13g
- Carb 5g
- Protein 13g

Herbed Baked Eggs

Prep time: 5 minutes	Cook time: 15 minutes	Servings: 4

Ingredients

- Minced fresh garlic – ¼ tsp.
- Minced fresh thyme leaves – ½ tsp.
- Minced fresh rosemary leaves – ½ tsp.
- Minced fresh parsley – 1 Tbsp.
- Freshly grated parmesan – 1 Tbsp.
- Eggs – 8 large
- Heavy cream – 2 Tbsp.
- Unsalted butter – 2 Tbsp.

- Kosher salt and ground black pepper
- Toasted almond bread for serving

Method

1. Preheat the broiler for 5 minutes.
2. Position the oven rack about 6 inches below the heat.
3. Mix the parmesan, parsley, rosemary, thyme, and garlic. Set aside.
4. Break 2 eggs into each of 4 bowls without breaking the yolks.
5. Place 4 individual ramekins on a baking sheet.
6. Place ½ tbsp. butter and ½ tbsp. cream in each dish.
7. Place under broiler until hot and bubbly, about 3 minutes.
8. Pour 2 eggs into each gratin dish. Then sprinkle evenly with herb mixture.
9. Then sprinkle with salt and pepper.
10. Place back under the broiler until the whites of the eggs are almost cooked, about 5 to 6 minutes.
11. Serve with toasted almond bread.

Nutritional Facts Per Serving (2 eggs, without bread)

- Calories 227
- Fat 19g
- Carb 1g
- Protein 13g

Pumpkin Pancakes

Prep time: 5 minutes	Cook time: 10 minutes	Servings: 4

Pancake ingredients

- Egg – 1, large
- Egg whites – 2
- Cream cheese – 2 Tbsp.
- Unsweetened, canned pumpkin – 3 Tbsp. (not pie filling)
- Vanilla extract – 1 Tbsp.

- Almond flour - 2/3 cup
- Coconut flour – 2 Tbsp.
- Swerve sweetener – 1 Tbsp. or another low carb sweetener
- Pumpkin pie spice – 1 tsp.
- Salt – 1/8 tsp.
- Baking powder – 1 tsp.
- Baking soda – ¼ tsp.
- Xanthan gum – ½ tsp.
- Water as needed

Topping

- Cream cheese – 1/3 cup
- Unsweetened canned pumpkin – 2 Tbsp.
- Swerve sweetener – 1 to 1 ½ Tbsp.
- Cinnamon – ½ tsp.
- Pumpkin pie spice – 1/8 tsp.
- Vanilla extract – ½ tsp.

Method

1. Preheat a griddle to 350F/180C. Except for the water, add all the wet pancake ingredients into a blender and blend. Then add the dry ingredients and blend until smooth.
2. A little at a time, add water until pancake batter has the right consistency.
3. In the preheated, oiled griddle, pour a small amount of batter.

4. Cook until browned and the edges almost to the center are dry, about 3 to 4 minutes.
5. Then flip and cook for another 2 to 3 minutes.
6. For the topping: in a processor, add all topping ingredients and blend until creamy.
7. Top the pancakes with toppings and drizzle with maple syrup.

Nutritional Facts Per Serving (3-inch)

- Calories 230
- Fat 16 g
- Carb 9.5 g
- Protein 8 g

Egg Squash and Avocado Spaghetti Boats

Prep time: 10 minutes	Cook time: 50 minutes	Servings: 2

Ingredients

- Spaghetti squash – 1 small, cut in half lengthwise, and seeds removed
- Salsa – 4 Tbsp. divided
- Avocado – 1, chopped and divided
- Eggs – 2 large

- No-sugar-added ketchup – 4 Tbsp. divided

Method

1. Preheat the oven to 400F/200C.
2. Line a baking sheet with parchment paper. Then place the squash, cut-side down, and bake for 30 minutes.
3. Remove from oven and cool for 15 minutes or until safe to touch.
4. Increase temperature to 425F/220C.
5. Separate spaghetti squash with a fork into strands, leaving them inside the shells.
6. To each half, add 2 Tbsp. salsa and mix gently with a fork.
7. Top with ½ avocado, and on each shell, break 1 egg.
8. For a fully baked egg, sink it more into the squash, and for runny egg yolk, break the egg on top.
9. Bake until the egg whites appear to be set, about 20 to 22 minutes.
10. Serve with ketchup.

Nutritional Facts Per Serving

- Calories 269.4
- Fat 16.1g
- Carb 5.4g
- Protein 8.5g

Keto Oatmeal

| Prep time: 10 minutes | Cook time: 5 minutes | Servings: 6 |

Ingredients

- Chia seeds - 1/3 cup
- Crushed pecans - 1 cup
- Cauliflower - 1/2 cup, riced
- Flaxseed meal - 1/3 cup
- Coconut milk - 3 1/2 cups
- Butter - 3 tbsp.
- Heavy cream - 1/4 cup
- Cream cheese - 3 oz.
- Maple flavor - 1 tsp.
- Cinnamon - 1 1/2 tsp.
- Erythritol - 3 tbsp. powdered

- Vanilla - 1/2 tsp.
- Allspice - 1/4 tsp.
- Nutmeg - 1/4 tsp.
- Liquid stevia - 10-15 drops
- Xanthan gum -1/8 tsp. (optional)

Method

- Heat coconut milk over medium heat in a pan.
- Crush pecans and add to the pan over low heat to toast.
- Now add cauliflower to the coconut milk and bring to a boil. Reduce to simmer, add spices, and mix.
- Grind erythritol and add to the pan. Then add chia seeds, flax, stevia and mix well.
- Add butter, cream, and cream cheese to the pan and mix well.
- Add xanthan gum to make it a bit thicker.
- Serve.

Nutritional Facts Per Serving

- Calories 398
- Fat 37.7g
- Carb 3.1g
- Protein 8.8g

Blueberry Ricotta Pancakes

Prep time: 10 minutes	Cook time: 10 minutes	Servings: 5

Ingredients

- Blueberries – ¼ cup
- Stevia powder – ¼ to ½ tsp.
- Baking powder – 1 tsp.
- Salt – ¼ tsp.
- Golden flaxseed meal – ½ cup
- Almond flour – 1 cup
- Unsweetened vanilla almond milk – ¼ cup
- Vanilla extract – ½ tsp.

- Ricotta – ¾ cup
- Eggs – 3 large

Method

1. Over high heat, preheat the skillet. In a bowl, blend the vanilla extract, unsweetened almond milk, ricotta, and eggs.
2. In another bowl, mix almond flour, golden flaxseed meal, baking powder, stevia, and salt.
3. Blend the dry ingredients into a smooth batter with a hand mixer. Add 2 to 3 blueberries per pancake.
4. Add the butter to the preheated skillet and let the butter melt.
5. Pour the batter into the skillet and flip when lightly browned on the outside. Cook both sides and repeat with the remaining batter.
6. Serve with sugar-free syrup and additional berries.

Nutritional Facts Per Serving

- Calories 296.6
- Fat 22.6g
- Carb 5.9g
- Protein 13.4g

Pancake Donuts

Prep time: 10 minutes	Cook time: 15 minutes	Servings: 22

Ingredients

- Liquid stevia – 10 drops
- Erythritol – 4 tbsp.
- Vanilla extract – 1 tsp.
- Baking powder – 1 tsp.
- Cooking flour – 1 tbsp.
- Almond flour – 4 tbsp.
- Egg – 3 large
- Cream cheese – 3 oz.

Method

1. With a hand mixer, blend all ingredients well.

2. Heat a donut maker. Then spray with oil.
3. Pour batter into the donut maker.
4. Cook 3 minutes, then flip and cook for 2 minutes more.
5. Remove the donuts from the donut maker and set them aside.
6. Repeat with the rest of the batter.
7. Serve.

Nutritional Facts Per Serving

- Calories 32
- Fat 2.7 g
- Carb 0.4g
- Protein 1.4g

Chapter 6

Lunch Recipes

Spicy Shrimp Rolls

| Prep time: 5 minutes | Cook time: 0 minutes | Servings: 5 |

Ingredients

- Cooked shrimp – 2 cups, chopped
- Mayonnaise – ¼ cup
- Sriracha – 1 Tbsp.
- Cilantro leaves – 2 Tbsp.
- Cucumber – ¼, julienned
- Hand roll nori sheets – 5

Method

1. In a bowl, combine the Sriracha sauce, mayonnaise, and chopped shrimp.
2. Layout one-hand roll sheets (the widest part is facing you).
3. On the right side of the wrap, place 1/3 of the shrimp mixture. The remaining 2/3 should remain empty.
4. Add cucumber strips, avocado, and cilantro leaves.
5. Roll on and make a cone.
6. Seal the edges with water.

Nutritional Facts Per Serving (1 roll)

- Calories 130
- Fat 10g
- Carb 1g

- Protein 9g

Zucchini Sardines Lunch

Prep time: 5 minutes	Cook time: 5 minutes	Servings: 2

Ingredients

- Brisling sardines packed in olive oil – 4 oz. can
- Extra-virgin olive oil – 1 Tbsp.
- Garlic – 1 tsp. chopped
- Ripe tomatoes – ½ cup, drained
- Zucchini noodles – 4 cups

- Capers – 1 Tbsp., drained
- Salt and pepper to taste
- Fresh parsley – 1 Tbsp. chopped

Method

1. In a large sauté pan, pour the oils from the sardine can and heat over medium heat. Add 1 Tbsp. olive oil.
2. Add the garlic and cook until fragrant, about 1 minute.
3. Add the tomatoes and capers and cook for 1 minute more.
4. Add the sardines and cook for one more minute.
5. Add the zucchini noodles and cook for 2 minutes. Stir gently.
6. Season with salt and pepper.
7. Garnish with parsley and serve.

Nutritional Facts Per Serving

- Calories 230
- Fat 19g
- Carb 6g
- Protein 10g

Keto Pizza (Pizza crust)

Prep time: 5 minutes	Cook time: 25 minutes	Servings: 4

Ingredients for the pizza crust

- Flax meals – 1 cup
- Finely grated parmesan cheese – ½ cup
- Eggs – 2

Method

1. In a bowl, mix the parmesan and flax meal.
2. Add the eggs and make a dough.
3. Wet your hands with water and then press onto greased cookie sheet (1/3 inch thick in a circle.) You should get a 10-inch crust.
4. Bake in the preheated 350F/180C oven for 8 minutes. Remove.
5. Add toppings and bake for 15 minutes more at 350F/180C.
6. Remove and cool.

Nutritional Facts Per Serving (¼ pizza, crust only)

- Calories 239

- Fat 18g

- Carb 0g

- Protein 13g

Pizza

| Prep time: 5 minutes | Cook time: 15 minutes | Servings: 4 |

Ingredients

- Pizza crust – 1 recipe
- Sugar-free marinara sauce – ½ cup
- Italian sausage link – 1, cooked and chopped
- Broccoli florets – ½ cup, cooked
- Mozzarella cheese – 1 cup, shredded

Method

1. To your pizza crust, add the toppings and bake at 350F/180C for 15 minutes.
2. Cut into 4 pieces.
3. Serve.

Nutritional Facts Per Serving

- Calories 381
- Fat 19g
- Carb 4g
- Protein 24g

Fish Cakes

Prep time: 30 minutes	Cook time: 10 minutes	Servings: 3

Ingredients

- Cauliflower puree – 2 cups
- Whitefish – 2 cups (cooked, flaked)
- Old boy seasoning – 2 tsp.
- Fresh cilantro – 1 Tbsp. chopped
- Scallions – 1 Tbsp. chopped

- Egg – 1 large
- Pork rinds – as much as needed
- Butter – 2 Tbsp. (for frying the cakes)

Method

1. In a bowl, combine the first 6 ingredients. Stir carefully, so the fish is not disturbed too much.
2. Chill for 30 minutes.
3. Remove from the fridge and make 6 patties. Chill again.
4. Dip into the pork rinds and sprinkle them on top.
5. In a nonstick pan, melt butter.
6. Cook patties until slightly puffed and golden brown, about 4 minutes per side.
7. Remove and serve with sauce.

Nutritional Facts Per Serving (1 cake)

- Calories 251
- Fat 18g
- Carb 8g
- Protein 14g

Cheddar Cheese Sandwich

Prep time: 5 minutes	Cook time: 6 minutes	Servings: 1

Ingredients

Bun

- Almond Flour - 2 Tbsp.
- Eggs - 2 large
- Soft Butter - 2 Tbsp.

- Psyllium Husk Powder - 1 ½ Tbsp.
- Baking Powder - ½ tsp.

Fillings and Extras

- Butter - 1 Tbsp. for frying
- Cheddar cheese - 2 oz.

Method

1. Mix all the bun ingredients in a bowl. Continue to mix until it thickens up.
2. Pour the mixture into a square bowl and level it off.
3. Bake in the microwave for 90 seconds and check if it is done. Cook for a few more minutes if needed.
4. When cooked, remove from the bowl, slice in half.
5. Place cheese between buns.
6. In a pan, heat butter over medium heat and fry the grilled cheese until it achieves your desired texture.

Nutritional Facts Per Serving

- Calorie 493
- Fat 40g
- Carb 4.7g
- Protein 29g

Chili with Italian Sausage

Prep time: 5 minutes	Cook time: 1 to 2 hours	Servings: 5

Ingredients

- Ground beef - 1 lb.
- Tomato Sauce - 1 can, no sugar added
- Hot Italian sausage - 1 lb.
- Yellow pepper - 1 Large, chopped
- Green pepper - 1 Large, chopped
- White onion - 1 medium, chopped
- Butter - 1 Tbsp.
- Chili powder - 2 Tbsp.

- Curry powder - 2 Tbsp.
- Coconut oil - 1 Tbsp.
- Minced garlic - 1 Tbsp.
- Cumin - 2 Tbsp.
- Onion powder - 1 tsp.
- Freshly ground black pepper - 1 tsp.
- Salt - 1 tsp.

Method

1. Dice onions, peppers, and minced garlic.
2. Add coconut oil and butter to the pan and heat over medium-high heat.
3. Once melted, add garlic, onions, and peppers. Sauté and stir.
4. Heat a pot over medium heat; add sausage and ground beef.
5. Cook the beef and sausage until browned. Season with salt and pepper.
6. Combine the garlic, peppers, and onion with the meat mixture.
7. Add chili powder, onion powder, and tomato sauce. Let cook for 20 minutes.
8. Add curry powder and cumin and cook for 10 minutes more, stirring often.
9. Simmer for 45 minutes to 2 hours. It depends on how thick you want the chili.

Nutritional Facts Per Serving

- Calorie 415
- Fat 25g
- Carb 6g
- Protein 29.2g

Bacon Chicken

| Prep time: 10 minutes | Cook time: 1 hour | Servings: 6 |

Ingredients

- Thyme – 1 tsp.
- Paprika – 1 tsp.
- Garlic powder – ½ tsp.
- Onion powder – ½ tsp.
- Sea salt – ½ tsp.
- Black pepper – ¼ tsp.
- Whole cut up chicken – 5 to 7 pieces
- Head of cabbage - ½, sliced

- Bacon – 5 slices
- Medium size parsnip – ½, sliced
- Medium onion – ½, chopped
- Garlic – 4 cloves, minced
- Chicken broth – 1/3 cup

Method

1. Preheat the oven to 375F/190C.
2. Add all the spice rub ingredients in a small bowl and stir.
3. In a large mixing bowl, add raw chicken and spice rub mix. Toss chicken to coat. Set aside.
4. In a large oven-safe skillet, fry bacon. Then remove and set on a plate with paper towels. Remove some bacon grease from the pan and leave some grease for the chicken. Chop the bacon slices and set them aside.
5. Add the chicken to the greased pan. Sear and brown on both sides on medium-high heat. Remove chicken from the pan when browned and set on a platter. Set aside.
6. Keep the heat on medium-high. Add cabbage to the skillet and stir. Then add sliced parsnips and chicken broth and stir. Add minced garlic and chopped onion and stir. Then add chopped bacon to the skillet and stir.
7. Remove from heat. Place the chicken pieces on top of the bacon-cabbage mixture in the skillet.
8. Place skillet in the oven and bake until chicken is done about 45 to 50 minutes.

Nutritional Facts Per Serving

- Calories 330
- Fat 20 g
- Carb 5 g
- Protein 24 g

Chapter 7

Dinner Recipes

Cheesy Cauliflower Casserole

Prep time: 10 minutes	Cook time: 40 minutes	Servings: 8

Ingredients

- Cauliflower florets – 8 cups, cooked and well-drained
- Sugar-free vodka sauce – 2 cups
- Heavy whipping cream – 2 Tbsp.
- Melted butter – 2 Tbsp.
- Grated Parmesan cheese – 1/3 cup
- Kosher salt – ½ tsp.
- Ground black pepper – ¼ tsp.
- Provolone cheese – 6 slices
- Fresh basil – ¼ cup, chopped

Method

1. In a large bowl, combine Parmesan cheese, kosher salt, black pepper, butter, heavy whipping cream, vodka sauce, and cauliflower. Toss to coat well.
2. Into a baking dish, transfer the mixture and top with slices of mozzarella or Provolone cheese.
3. Bake in the preheated oven at 375F/190C until the cheese is completely melted and the casserole is bubbling, about 30 to 40 minutes.
4. Remove from the oven and let it rest for 10 minutes.
5. Top with basil and serve.

Nutritional Facts Per Serving

- Calories 214
- Fat 14g
- Carb 6g
- Protein 12g

Skillet Chicken and Mushrooms

Prep time: 10 minutes	Cook time: 25 minutes	Servings: 4

Ingredients

- Butter – ¼ cup
- Mushrooms – 2 cups, sliced
- Chicken thighs – 4 large
- Onion powder – ½ tsp.
- Garlic powder – ½ tsp.

- Kosher salt – 1 tsp.
- Black pepper – ¼ tsp.
- Water – ½ cup
- Dijon mustard – 1 tsp.
- Fresh tarragon – 1 tbsp., chopped

Method

1. Season the chicken thighs with onion powder, garlic powder, salt, and pepper.
2. In a heavy-bottomed sauté pan, melt 1 tbsp. butter.
3. Sear the chicken thighs for about 3 to 4 minutes per side, or until both sides are golden brown. Remove the thighs from the pan.
4. Add the remaining 3 tbsp. of butter to the pan and melt.
5. Add the mushrooms and cook for 4 to 5 minutes, or until golden brown. Stirring as little as possible.
6. Add the Dijon mustard and water to the pan. Stir to deglaze.
7. Place the chicken thighs back to the pan, keep the skin side up.
8. Cover and simmer until chicken is cooked through, about 15 minutes.
9. Stir in the fresh herbs, let sit for 5 minutes and serve.

Nutritional Facts Per Serving

- Calories 447
- Fat 31g

- Carb 1g
- Protein 37g

Pan-Seared Steaks

Prep time: 5 minutes	Cook time: 10 minutes	Servings: 1

Ingredients

- Steak (filet, sirloin strip, ribeye) – 6 oz. (about 1 inch thick)
- Salted butter – 2 Tbsp.
- Sliced shiitake mushrooms – ½ cup
- Kosher salt and pepper to taste

Method

1. Heat a cast-iron pan on medium heat for 1 minute.

2. Season the steak with salt and pepper and add to the hot pan.
3. Cook for 3 to 4 minutes for medium-rare.
4. Remove the steak to a plate.
5. Add butter and mushrooms to the pan.
6. Cook until the mushrooms are golden brown, about 3 to 4 minutes. Remove from the heat.
7. Season the mushroom with salt and pepper if needed.
8. Add the steak back to the pan and baste in the butter.
9. Allow to rest in the warm butter for a couple of minutes.
10. Slice and serve.

Nutritional Facts Per Serving

- Calories 370
- Fat 29g
- Carb 3g
- Protein 35g

Low Carb Chori Pollo

| Prep time: 10 minutes | Cook time: 25 to 30 minutes | Servings: 6 |

Ingredients

- Sliced onions – 1 cup
- Butter – 2 Tbsp.
- Shredded turkey meat – 3 cups, cooked

- Mexican chorizo – 8 oz. raw
- Ground coriander – ½ tsp.
- Ground cumin – ½ tsp.
- Garlic powder – ½ tsp.
- Chipotle powder – ½ tsp.
- Cheddar cheese – 1 cup

Method

1. In a sauté pan, melt the butter and add the onions. Season with salt and pepper and cook on low-medium heat until caramelized and golden, about 7 to 10 minutes. Remove from pan and set aside.
2. Add the chorizo to the pan and cook until cooked through, about 5 minutes. Remove and set aside.
3. Add the shredded turkey to the pan along with chipotle powder, garlic powder, cumin, and coriander. Season with salt and pepper to taste. Heat for 3 to 5 minutes.
4. Assemble Chori Pollo: in an oven-proof casserole dish, spread the chicken (about 1-inch depth). Over the top of the chicken, sprinkle the chorizo evenly. Then spread the onions and sprinkle the shredded cheese over the top.
5. Bake at 375F/190C until the cheese has melted, about 10 minutes.
6. Serve hot with sour cream.

Nutritional Facts Per Serving (¾ cup)

- Calories 405

- Fat 30g
- Carb 3g
- Protein 37g

Chicken, Bacon, and Cream Cheese Casserole

Prep time: 10 minutes	Cook time: 1 hour	Servings: 6

Ingredients

- Jalapenos - 3 medium (De-seed if you want)
- Chicken thighs - 6 small
- Bacon - 6 slices
- Hot sauce - 1/4 cup
- Shredded cheddar - 4 oz.

- Cream cheese - 12 oz.
- Shredded mozzarella cheese - 2 oz.
- Mayonnaise - 1/4 cup
- Salt and pepper to taste

Method

1. Preheat the oven to 400F/200C.
2. De-bone the chicken thighs and season with salt and pepper. Place them on a cooling rack over a cookie sheet wrapped in foil.
3. Bake the chicken for 40 minutes at 400F/200C.
4. While the chicken thighs are cooking, start on the filling.
5. Place a pan over medium heat, chop 6 slices of bacon into pieces, and put in the pan. Add jalapenos in the pan when bacon is almost crispy.
6. When jalapenos are cooked and soft, add cream cheese, mayo, and hot sauce to the pan. Mix well and season to taste.
7. Remove the chicken from the oven and allow it to cool slightly. Remove the skins when they are cool enough to handle.
8. Place chicken in the casserole dish and spread Cream cheese-jalapeno mixture over it. Top with cheddar and mozzarella.
9. Bake in the oven for 10 to 15 minutes at 400F/200C. Broil for 3 to 5 minutes to finish cooking.
10. If you want, top with extra jalapenos before you broil.

Nutritional Facts Per Serving

- Calorie 740
- Fat 61.2g
- Carb 2.5g
- Protein 31.8g

Feta-Stuffed Turkey Meatloaf

Prep time: 20 minutes	Cook time: 1 hour	Servings: 8

Ingredients for the Tzatziki sauce

- Full-fat Greek yogurt – ½ cup
- Lemon juice – 1 Tbsp.
- Garlic – 1 clove, minced
- Medium cucumber – 1/2 sliced
- Chopped fresh dill – 1 tsp.

- Salt – ¼ tsp.

Meatloaf

- Ground turkey – 2 lbs.
- Frozen spinach – 8 ounces, thawed and squeeze out
- Almond flour – ½ cup
- Eggs – 2
- Chopped onion – ¼ cup
- Salt – 1 tsp.
- Dried marjoram – 1 tsp.
- Freshly ground pepper – ¾ tsp.
- Crumble feta cheese – 1 cup

Method

1. To make the sauce, mix everything in a bowl. Keep in the refrigerator.
2. To make the meatloaf: Preheat the oven to 325F/160C. Line a rimmed baking sheet with parchment paper.
3. In a bowl, combine pepper, marjoram, salt, onion, eggs, almond flour, spinach, and turkey. Mix with hands and combine well.
4. On the prepared baking sheet, place ½ of the mixture and shape into a flat rectangle (about 1 inch thick).
5. Top with about ¾ cup of feta cheese.
6. Add the remaining turkey mixture on top of feta. Shape into a rough loaf.

7. Sprinkle with remaining feta and press lightly.
8. Bake until the internal temperature reaches 160F/70C, about 1 to 1 ¼ hours.
9. Slice and drizzle with tzatziki sauce.
10. Serve.

Nutritional Facts Per Serving

- Calories: 345
- Fat: 22.8g
- Carb: 5.9g
- Protein: 27.2g

Shrimp & Bacon Chowder

| Prep time: 5 minutes | Cook time: 25 minutes | Servings: 6 |

Ingredients

- Bacon – 6 slices, chopped
- Medium turnip – 1, cut into ½ cubes
- Chopped onion – ½ cup
- Garlic – 2 cloves, minced
- Chicken broth – 2 cups
- Heavy whipping cream – 1 cup

- Shrimp – 1 pound, peeled and deveined
- Cajun seasoning – ½ tsp.
- Salt and pepper
- Chopped parsley for garnish

Method

1. Cook bacon in a Dutch oven until crisp. Remove and drain on paper towels. Reserve the bacon fat in the pan.
2. Add the onion and turnip and sauté for 5 minutes, or until the onion is tender. Add garlic and cook until fragrant.
3. Pour in chicken broth and simmer for 10 minutes.
4. Add shrimp and cream and simmer for another 3 minutes, or until shrimp is cooked through.
5. Add Cajun seasoning and season with salt and pepper.
6. Garnish with chopped parsley and bacon and serve.

Nutritional Facts Per Serving

- Calories: 391
- Fat: 31.1g
- Carb: 5.6g
- Protein: 16.5g

Grilled Ribeye Steak with Butter Sauce

| Prep time: 5 minutes | Cook time: 8 to 15 minutes | Servings: 5 |

Ingredients

- Prime Ribeye Steaks – 2
- Salt and pepper

For the Butter sauce

- Butter – ½ cup, softened
- Gorgonzola cheese – 2 oz.
- Chopped parsley – ¼ cup
- Garlic – 1 clove, crushed

Method

1. Season the steaks with salt and pepper on both sides.
2. Grill on high heat until the desired temperature, about 4 to 5 minutes on each side for medium-rare.
3. Top with chilled butter. Allow to rest five minutes before serving.
4. For the Gorgonzola butter: in a food processor, combine the gorgonzola, butter, parsley, and garlic. Pulse to combine well. Chill.

Nutritional Facts Per Serving (6 oz. serving)

- Calories 450
- Fat 35g
- Carb 0g
- Protein 30g

Butter sauce – 2 Tbsp. serving

- Calories: 170
- Fat 18g
- Carb .5g
- Protein 2g

Chapter 8

Snack Recipes

Popcorn Chicken

| Prep time: 10 minutes | Cook time: 18 minutes | Servings: 6 |

Ingredients for the chicken

- Chicken breast or tenderloins – 2 lbs., cut into bite-sized pieces
- Almond flour – 1 cup
- Grated Parmesan – ¼ cup
- Ranch salad dressing and seasoning mix – 1 packet
- Mayonnaise – ½ cup
- Dijon mustard – 1 tsp.

For the dipping sauce

- Mayonnaise – 1/3 cup
- Dijon mustard – ¼ cup
- Sugar-free pancake syrup – ¼ cup

Method

1. To make the chicken: in a medium bowl, combine the ranch salad dressing and seasoning mix, cheese, and almond flour.
2. In another bowl, combine the mustard, mayonnaise, and chicken pieces. Stir well.
3. Dip the coated chicken pieces in the dry mixture and place them on a parchment-lined cookie sheet.

4. Bake the chicken at 400F/200C until cooked through and golden brown, about 15 to 18 minutes.
5. For the dipping sauce: in a bowl, combine the ingredients and whisk until smooth.
6. Serve.

Nutritional Facts Per Serving (5 oz. chicken)

- Calories 351
- Fat 20g
- Carb 4g
- Protein 40g

Sauce 2 tbsp.

- Calories 110
- Fat 12g
- Carb 0g
- Protein 0g

Tuna Jam

| Prep time: 10 minutes | Cook time: 0 minutes | Servings: 12 |

Ingredients

- Albacore tuna – 2 (6 oz.) cans
- Smoked tuna – 1 (6 oz.) can
- Sugar-free mayonnaise – 1/3 cup
- Dehydrated onion flakes – 1 tbsp.
- Garlic powder – ¼ tsp.
- Ground black pepper – ¼ tsp.
- Whole dill pickles – 6 large, cut in ½ and seeds removed

Method

1. Except for the pickles, combine all the ingredients in a bowl and mix well,
2. Fill each pickle half,
3. Chill and serve.

Nutritional Facts Per Serving (1 tuna pickle)

- Calories: 118
- Fats: 7g
- Carb: 1.5g
- Protein: 11g

Onion Rings

Prep time: 10 minutes	Cook time: 10 minutes	Servings: 4

Ingredients

- Onion – 1 large
- Egg – 1
- Coconut flour – 2 tbsp.
- Grated Parmesan cheese – 2 tbsp.
- Garlic powder – 1/8 tsp.

- Parsley flakes – ¼ tsp.
- Cayenne pepper – 1/8 tsp.
- Salt and pepper
- Olive oil – ¼ cup for frying

Method

1. In a sauté pan, heat the oil.
2. Meanwhile, in a bowl, beat the egg. Combine the cayenne, parsley flakes, garlic powder, parmesan, salt, and coconut flour.
3. Slice the onion about ½ to ¾ of an inch and make a big pile.
4. Dip the onion rings in the beaten egg. Soak the onions in the egg for at least 1 minute. Coat well.
5. Then dip in the coating in small batches and add to the hot oil.
6. Fry until golden brown. Then turn and brown on the other side. Place on a plate lined with a paper towel.
7. Serve with sugar-free ketchup.

Nutritional Facts Per Serving

- Calories 175
- Fat 16g
- Carb 4g
- Protein 3g

Mediterranean Deviled Eggs

Prep time: 10 minutes	Cook time: 0 minutes	Servings: 24

Ingredients

- Large eggs – 12, boiled
- Mayonnaise – ½ cup
- Dijon mustard – 1 tsp.
- Capers – 1 tbsp., chopped

- Kalamata olives – 1 tbsp., pitted and chopped
- Sundried tomatoes – 1 tbsp., chopped
- Olive oil – 1 tbsp.
- Fresh basil – 2 tbsp., minced
- Caper brine – 1 tsp.
- Salt and pepper to taste

Method

1. Sliced the eggs in half and remove the yolks.
2. Place the yolks in a bowl and mash with a fork.
3. In a food processor, combine the caper brine, basil, olive oil, sundried tomatoes, olives, capers, mustard, and mayonnaise. Blend until mostly smooth.
4. Fold the olive-tomato mixture into the egg yolks until smooth.
5. Season with salt and pepper.
6. Spoon into egg white halves.
7. Serve.

Nutritional Facts Per Serving (1 deviled egg half)

- Calories 78
- Fat 7g
- Carb 0g
- Protein 3g

Bacon Jalapeno Fat Bombs

Prep time: 5 minutes	Cook time: 0 minutes	Servings: 6

Ingredients

- Bacon - 5 slices, cooked, fat reserved
- Cream cheese - ¼ cup plus 2 Tbsp.
- Reserved bacon fat - 2 Tbsp.
- Seeded and finely chopped jalapeno pepper - 1 tsp.
- Finely chopped cilantro - 1 Tbsp.

Method

1. Chop bacon into small crumbs.

2. In a bowl, combine cilantro, jalapeno, bacon fat, and cream cheese. Mix well.

3. Form mixture into 6 balls.

4. Place bacon crumbles on a medium plate and roll balls through to coat evenly.

5. Serve.

Nutritional Facts Per Serving

- Calories: 132
- Fat: 11.5g
- Carb: 1g
- Protein: 4.1g

Smoked Salmon and Avocado Fat Bombs

| Prep time: 5 minutes | Cook time: 0 minutes | Servings: 3 |

Ingredients

- Medium avocado - ½, peeled and pitted
- Fresh lemon juice - 1 tsp.
- Sea salt - 1/8 tsp.

- Smoked salmon - 3 slices (1-ounce each)

Method

1. In a bowl, combine lemon juice, avocado, and salt. Mash with a fork.
2. Spread 1/3 avocado mixture evenly on top of each salmon slice.
3. Roll slices into individual rolls and secure with a toothpick.
4. Serve.

Nutritional Facts Per Serving

- Calories: 71
- Fat: 4.2g
- Carb: 2.1g
- Protein: 5.6g

Cocoa Coconut Butter Fat Bombs

Prep time: 5 minutes	Cook time: 10 minutes	Servings: 12

Ingredients

- Coconut oil - 1 cup
- Unsalted butter - ½ cup
- Unsweetened cocoa powder - 6 Tbsp.
- Liquid stevia - 15 drops
- Coconut butter - ½ cup

Method

1. In a saucepan, put butter, coconut oil, cocoa powder, and stevia and cook over low heat. Stirring frequently until melted.
2. Melt coconut butter in another saucepan over low heat.
3. Pour 2 Tbsp. of the cocoa mixture into each well of a 12 cup silicone mold.
4. Add 1 Tbsp. of melted coconut butter to each well.
5. Place in the freezer until hardened, about 30 minutes.
6. Serve.

Nutritional Facts Per Serving

- Calories: 297
- Fat: 30.6g
- Carb: 3.6g
- Protein: 1.3g

Raspberry Cheesecake Fat Bombs

| Prep time: 5 minutes | Cook time: 0 minutes | Servings: 12 |

Ingredients

- Frozen raspberries - ½ cup
- Liquid stevia - 10 drops

- Vanilla extract - 1 tsp.
- Cream cheese - 6 ounces, softened
- Coconut oil - ¼ cup, softened

Method

1. Process raspberries in a food processor until smooth. Add vanilla extract and stevia and process until mixed.
2. Add coconut oil and cream cheese and process until mixed.
3. Fill 12-cup silicone mold with the mixture.
4. Place in the freezer to harden, about 30 minutes.
5. Serve.

Nutritional Facts Per Serving

- Calories: 91
- Fat: 8.4g
- Carb: 1.3g
- Protein: 1g

Chapter 9

Side Dishes

Cheesy Zucchini Casserole

Prep time: 10 minutes	Cook time: 35 minutes	Servings: 6

Ingredients

- Medium zucchini – 2, chopped
- Butter – 2 Tbsp. cut into small pieces
- Large eggs – 3
- Heavy cream – ¼ cup
- Chopped onion - ¼ cup
- Salt – ½ tsp.
- Pepper – ½ tsp.
- Shredded cheddar – 6 ounces, divided
- Grated Parmesan cheese – ¼ cup
- Pork rinds – ¼ cup, finely crushed

Method

1. Cook zucchini in a large pot of lightly salted water for 4 minutes or until tender. Drain.
2. Preheat the oven to 350F/180C. Grease a baking dish.
3. Spread the zucchini in the baking dish and drizzle with butter.
4. Whisk the cream and eggs in a bowl. Stir in half the cheddar cheese, salt, pepper, and onions. Pour the mixture over the zucchini.

5. Sprinkle the top with pork rinds, parmesan, and remaining cheddar.
6. Bake until bubbly, about 35 minutes.
7. Sprinkle with chopped basil and serve.

Nutritional Facts Per Serving

- Calories: 195
- Fat: 14.4g
- Carb: 2.8g
- Protein: 10.4g

Cilantro Lime Cauliflower Rice

Prep time: 5 minutes	Cook time: 10 minutes	Servings: 4

Ingredients

- Riced cauliflower – 16 ounces
- Butter – 2 Tbsp.
- Salt – ½ tsp.
- Pepper – ¼ tsp.
- Chipotle powder – ½ tsp.

- Chopped cilantro – 3 tbsp.
- Lime juice – 2 Tbsp.
- Salt and pepper to taste

Method

1. Melt the butter in a skillet. Add cauliflower and coat with butter.
2. Sprinkle with a little chipotle powder, salt, and pepper. Stir-fry for 5 minutes, or until starting to brown.
3. Remove from heat and add lime juice, and chopped cilantro. Adjust salt and pepper to taste.
4. Serve.

Nutritional Facts Per Serving

- Calories: 79
- Fat: 5.6g
- Carb: 6.1g
- Protein: 2.2g

Creamy Avocado & Bacon Zoodles

Prep time: 5 minutes	Cook time: 2 minutes	Servings: 4

Ingredients

- Avocado – 1 ripe
- Chopped jalapeno – 1, seeds removed
- Garlic – 1 clove
- Lime juice – 2 Tbsp.
- Chopped fresh cilantro – 2 Tbsp.
- Avocado oil – 1 Tbsp.
- Chipotle powder – 1/8 tsp.
- Salt and pepper to taste
- Water – 2 to 4 Tbsp.

- Medium zucchini – 4
- Bacon – 4 slices, cooked crisp and crumbled

Method

1. In a food processor, combine the avocado oil, salt, pepper, chipotle powder, cilantro, lime juice, garlic, jalapeno, and avocado. Blend until smooth. Add a few tbsp. of water at a time and continue to blend until you get a thick paste.
2. Cut zucchini and cook uncovered in a microwave until just tender, about 1 to 2 minutes.
3. Arrange zucchini between 4 plates and top with jalapeno-avocado mixture and crumbled bacon.
4. Serve warm.

Nutritional Facts Per Serving

- Calories: 230
- Fat: 21.72g
- Carb: 8g
- Protein: 10g

Pesto Zucchini Lasagna Rolls

| Prep time: 20 minutes | Cook time: 45 minutes | Servings: 6 |

Ingredients

- Medium zucchini – 3, slice lengthwise into ¼ inch thick slices
- Avocado or olive oil – 1 Tbsp.
- Garlic – 2 cloves, minced
- Chopped spinach – 4 ounces
- Full fat ricotta – 1 cup

- Grated parmesan – ½ cup
- Egg – 1
- Salt – ¾ tsp.
- Pepper – ½ tsp.
- Pesto – ¼ cup
- Grated mozzarella – 1 cup

Method

1. Preheat a grill pan or a grill on medium.
2. Grill zucchini slices on the grill, 3 to 5 minutes per side, or until tender. Set aside on a paper towel.
3. Preheat the oven to 350F/180C. Then lightly grease a 9 x 12-inch baking dish.
4. Heat oil in a skillet. Add garlic and stir-fry for 30 seconds. Add spinach and cook until just wilted.
5. In a bowl, combine salt, pepper, egg, parmesan, and ricotta. Add spinach mixture and mix well.
6. Spread half of each zucchini slice with 1 tbsp. ricotta filling. Roll and place in the baking dish. Repeat with the remaining filling and zucchini.
7. Spread pesto over zucchini rolls and sprinkle with mozzarella.
8. Bake until cheese is bubbling, about 30 minutes.

Nutritional Facts Per Serving

- Calories: 224

- Fat: 16.71g
- Carb: 7g
- Protein: 13.32g

Easy Pan Pizza

| Prep time: 20 minutes | Cook time: 35 minutes | Servings: 12 |

Ingredients

- Almond flour – 2 cups
- Coconut flour – ¼ cup
- Baking powder – 2 tsp.
- Garlic powder – 1 tsp.
- Salt – ½ tsp.

- Eggs - 3
- Olive oil – ½ cup
- Unsweetened almond milk – ½ cup

Toppings

- Sugar-free tomato sauce – 1 cup
- Pepperoni slices – 3 ounces
- Shredded mozzarella – 1 ½ cups

Method

1. Preheat the oven to 325F/160C and grease a baking pan 9 x 13.
2. In a bowl, whisk together the flours, salt, garlic powder, and baking powder. Stir in oil, eggs, and almond milk until mixed well.
3. Spread the mixture evenly into the prepared baking pan.
4. Bake until golden around the edges, about 18 to 22 minutes.
5. Toppings: spread the tomato sauce on top of the warm crust. Top with cheese and pepperoni.
6. Bake again until cheese is bubbly and melted, about 10 minutes more.
7. Finally, turn on the broiler for a few minutes to brown the cheese.
8. Serve.

Nutritional Facts Per Serving

- Calories: 214

- Fat: 16.91g
- Carb: 8.77g
- Protein: 10g

Roasted Broccoli & Bacon Alfredo

Prep time: 10 minutes	Cook time: 35 minutes	Servings: 8

Ingredients

- Broccoli florets – 8 cups
- Avocado oil – ¼ cup
- Salt – 1 tsp.
- Pepper – ½ tsp.
- Butter – 2 Tbsp.
- Garlic – 2 cloves, minced
- Heavy cream – 1 cup
- Pepper – 1/8 tsp.
- Salt to taste

- Grated parmesan cheese – ½ cup
- Bacon – 6 slices, cooked and crumbled

Method

1. Preheat the oven to 350F/180C. Line a baking sheet with parchment paper.
2. In a bowl, mix oil, broccoli, salt, and pepper. Spread on the baking sheet in a single layer.
3. Roast for 20 to 30 minutes.
4. Melt butter in a saucepan. Add garlic and sauté for 30 seconds.
5. Lower heat, add the salt, pepper, and cream, and bring to a simmer.
6. Add Parmesan and cook for 3 to 4 minutes, or until thickened.
7. Add the bacon and broccoli and stir to combine.
8. Serve.

Nutritional Facts Per Serving

- Calories: 247
- Fat: 23.9g
- Carb: 7.4g
- Protein: 7.39g

Lemongrass Chicken with Cauliflower Rice

Prep time: 5 minutes	Cook time: 25 minutes	Servings: 4

Ingredients for the rice

- Avocado oil – 2 Tbsp.
- Cauliflower – 1 large head, riced
- Salt – ½ tsp.
- Pepper – ½ tsp.
- Dried cilantro – 1 Tbsp.

Lemongrass chicken

- Fish sauce – 1 Tbsp.

- Garlic paste – 3 tsp.
- Sea salt – ½ tsp.
- Boneless skinless chicken thighs – 1 ½ lb. cut into bite-sized pieces
- Swerve sweetener – 2 Tbsp.
- Water – 2 Tbsp. divided
- Avocado oil – 2 Tbsp.
- Lemongrass paste – 3 Tbsp.
- Red chili to taste

Method

1. Heat oil in a skillet.
2. Add riced cauliflower and season with salt and pepper. Toss to coat with oil. Stir-fry for 5 minutes, or until tender-crisp.
3. Add cilantro paste and stir to combine. Cook 1 minute more. Remove from heat and set aside.
4. To make the lemongrass chicken: in a bowl, combine garlic paste, sea salt, and fish sauce. Add chicken and toss to combine.
5. In a skillet, combine 1 tbsp. water and swerve. Stir until the swerve is dissolved. Bring to a boil and cook until golden caramel color. Add the remaining water and set it aside.
6. Heat oil in another skillet. Add chili paste and lemongrass paste and stir-fry for 1 minute.
7. Add chicken and stir-fry until mostly cooked. Add the caramel mixture and cook until you get a thick sauce.

8. Serve chicken over cauliflower rice.

Nutritional Facts Per Serving

- Calories: 323
- Fat: 15.g
- Carb: 9g
- Protein: 36g

Mushroom and Spinach

| Prep time: 10 minutes | Cook time: 10 minutes | Servings: 4 |

Ingredients

- Spinach leaves – 10 ounces, chopped
- Salt and ground black pepper to taste
- Mushrooms – 14 ounces, chopped
- Garlic – 2 cloves, minced
- Fresh parsley – ½ cup, chopped

- Onion – 1, chopped
- Olive oil – 4 Tbsp.
- Balsamic vinegar – 2 Tbsp.

Method

1. Heat oil in a pan. Add garlic and onion and stir-fry for 4 minutes.
2. Add mushrooms and stir-fry for 3 minutes more.
3. Add spinach and stir-fry for 3 more minutes.
4. Add salt, pepper, and vinegar and cook for 1 minute.
5. Add parsley and mix.
6. Divide between plates and serve.

Nutritional Facts Per Serving

- Calories: 175
- Fat: 14.7g
- Carb: 5.8g
- Protein: 9.4g

Chapter 10

Desserts

Coconut Cake

Prep time: 20 minutes	Cook time: 50 minutes	Servings: 4

Ingredients

For the cake layer

- Cream cheese – 4 oz. softened
- Eggs – 3
- Coconut cream – 1 tbsp.
- Sugar-free coconut-flavored syrup – 1 tbsp.
- Coconut flour – 2 tbsp.

For the coconut filling

- Dried unsweetened coconut – 1 cup
- Coconut cream – ½ cup
- Sugar-free coconut-flavored syrup – 3 tbsp.

For the frosting

- Heavy whipping cream – 1 cup
- Sugar-free coconut-flavored syrup – 1 tbsp.
- Stevia powder – 1 tsp.
- Coconut cream – ¼ cup

Method

1. To make the cake: in a blender, combine all of the ingredients and blend until smooth. Let it rest for a few minutes if it is frothy.
2. Then into a greased 8 x 8 microwave-safe dish, pour ½.
3. Cook in the microwave until firm, about 3 minutes.
4. Flip out the dish onto a cutting board.
5. Grease again and repeat with the remaining batter.
6. Cut into squares, so you get 9 squares per pan or 18 squares total.
7. For the filling: in a bowl, combine all the ingredients and let sit for about ten minutes before using. It will help to absorb all of the liquid.
8. For the frosting: whip the heavy cream almost completely before adding the stevia, syrup, and coconut cream. Keep whipping until the cream holds its shape easily.
9. To assemble: on each plate, lay one square of cake and place 1 tbsp. filling in the center of each square.
10. Spread to the edges and then cover with another square of the cake. Repeat until the finish.
11. Use whipped cream to frost the top cake layer and sides.

Nutritional Facts Per Serving

- Calories 543
- Fat 51 g
- Carb 7 g

- Protein 11 g

Chocolate Peanut Butter Chocolate Cups

Prep time: 15 minutes	Cook time: 10 minutes	Servings: 12

Ingredients

- Coconut oil – ¾ cup
- Cocoa powder – ¼ cup
- Peanut butter – ¼ cup
- Coconut oil – 1 tsp.
- Liquid stevia – 30 drops

Method

1. Heat ¾ cup coconut oil until melted. Then divide into 3 bowls.

2. In one bowl of oil, stir in the cocoa powder until completely dissolved.
3. Add about 6 drops of liquid stevia. Stir to mix.
4. In another bowl of oil, add the peanut butter. Blend until smooth. Add 6 drops of liquid stevia.
5. In the last bowl, add the 1 tsp. coconut oil. Add the remaining liquid stevia.
6. Divide the chocolate mixture into 12 small cups.
7. Refrigerate for 10 minutes or until firm.
8. When firm, divide the peanut butter mixture over the chocolate mixture.
9. Return to the fridge until set.
10. When firm, divide the coconut oil mixture over the hard peanut butter layer.
11. Chill until firm and serve.

Nutritional Facts Per Serving

- Calories: 153
- Fat: 16.6g
- Carb: 2.1g
- Protein: 1.7g

Avocado Chocolate Pudding Pops

Prep time: 15 minutes	Cook time: 0 minutes	Servings: 10

Ingredients

- Unsweetened coconut milk – 6 Tbsp.
- Coconut oil – 2 Tbsp.
- Cocoa powder – 2 Tbsp.
- Avocado – 2 ripe
- Unsweetened chocolate – 2 ounces, chopped
- Stevia extract – ¼ tsp.
- Low-carb powdered sweetener - ¼ cup
- Vanilla extract – ½ tsp.
- Pinch salt

Method

1. Puree the avocado in a blender until smooth.
2. Add the sweetener, cocoa powder, coconut milk, stevia extract, vanilla, and salt. Continue processing on low until well mixed.
3. Melt the coconut oil and chocolate together in a microwave until smooth.
4. Spoon ½ of the mixture into popsicle molds and then tap the molds on a hard flat surface to release air bubbles.
5. Spoon the remaining mixture into the mold. Tap once again.
6. Press wooden Popsicle sticks into the mold, about 2/3 deep.
7. Freeze until set.
8. Serve.

Nutritional Facts Per Serving

- Calories: 197
- Fat: 19.8g
- Carb: 5.4g
- Protein: 2.4g

Chocolate Truffles

Prep time: 10 minutes	Cook time: 0 minute	Servings: 12

Ingredients

- Ripe Hass avocados – 2, pitted and skinned
- Coconut oil – 2 Tbsp.
- Premium cocoa powder – ½ cup
- Granulated sugar substitute – 1 Tbsp.
- Sugar-free chocolate-flavored syrup – 2 Tbsp.

- Heavy whipping cream – 2 Tbsp.
- Bourbon – 2 Tbsp.
- Chopped pecans – ½ cup

Method

1. Except for the pecans, combine all ingredients in a small blender and process until smooth. Chill until firm enough to work with, about 1 hour.
2. Make 1-inch balls and then roll in the pecans.
3. Chill until firm and store in the refrigerator.

Nutritional Facts Per Serving (1 truffle)

- Calories 111
- Fat 10g
- Carb 4.5g
- Protein 1.5g

Almond Joy Cookies

| Prep time: 10 minutes | Cook time: 20 minutes | Servings: 18 |

Ingredients

- Almond butter – 2 Tbsp.
- Coconut oil – 1 Tbsp.
- Coconut milk – ¼ cup
- Sugar-free coconut syrup – 2 Tbsp.
- Eggs – 2 large
- Baking powder – ½ tsp.

- Salt – ½ tsp.
- Granulated sugar substitute – 2 Tbsp.
- Sugar-free dried coconut – 1 ½ cup
- Flax meal – ½ cup
- 90% dark chocolate – 2 squares
- Almond – 18

Method

1. In a bowl, combine the coconut oil and almond butter and mix well.
2. Add the eggs, syrup, and coconut milk and mix until smooth.
3. Stir in the flax meal, dried coconut, sweetener, salt, and baking powder.
4. Roll the dough into 18 (1-inch) balls and place on a parchment-covered cookie sheet.
5. Press lightly to make a dent on each ball.
6. Top with chopped chocolate (each cookie) and top with an almond.
7. Bake in a preheated 375F/190C oven until browned and slightly puffed, about 20 minutes.
8. Serve.

Nutritional Facts Per Serving (1 cookie)

- Calories 114
- Fat 11g
- Carb 4g

- Protein 3g

Hawaiian Cookies

Prep time: 10 minutes	Cook time: 15 minutes	Servings: 24

Ingredients

- Almond flour – 1 ¼ cup
- Coconut flour – 1 Tbsp.
- Unsweetened shredded coconut – ¼ cup
- Baking powder - 1 ½ tsp.

- Sea salt – ¼ tsp.
- Erythritol – 2/3 cup plus ½ tbsp. powdered
- Butter – 6 tbsp.
- Egg – 1 large
- Vanilla extract – ½ tsp.
- Low carb chocolate chips – 1/3 cup
- Chopped macadamia nuts – ¼ cup

Method

1. Preheat the oven to 325F/160C. Line a baking sheet with parchment paper.
2. In a bowl, beat erythritol and cream butter with a hand mixer until well combined.
3. Add vanilla extract and egg to the mixing bowl and mix until combined.
4. In another bowl, combine shredded coconut, coconut flour, almond flour, baking powder, and sea salt. Stir until combined.
5. Add the dry ingredients to the wet ingredients and mix in until combined.
6. Fold in macadamia nuts and chocolate chips.
7. On the prepared baking sheet, place tbsp. size spoonful of batter, 1 ½ inch apart.
8. Bake until cookies are browned on the bottoms, about 12 to 15 minutes.

9. Remove and cool until the cookies firm up and set, at least 25 minutes.

Nutritional Facts Per Serving

- Calories 82
- Fat 8 g
- Carb 2.8 g
- Protein 2 g

Conclusion

The Ketogenic diet is a proven weight loss diet. Many overweight and obese people are eager to follow this diet and shred unwanted body weight. However, only a few succeed because of a lack of proper guidance. This book on the Ketogenic diet is a comprehensive guide and gives you all the important information you need to know to make the diet a success.

Start today!

Thank you for giving your attention and time to read my book. I am very pleased if this book will help you to achieve the healthy lifestyle which you desire. It means a lot to me and I wish you the very best in your journey.

Did you enjoy my book? If you could take a second and leave a review, I would really appreciate it! I love hearing your thoughts, genuine feedback really helps readers find out the pros of the Keto diet.

Thank you.